for Kids

GOD'S LITTLE INSTRUCTION BOOK FOR KIDS, MINI EDITION
Published by David C Cook
4050 Lee Vance View
Colorado Springs, CO 80918 U.S.A.

David C Cook Distribution Canada
55 Woodslee Avenue, Paris, Ontario, Canada N3L 3E5

David C Cook U.K., Kingsway Communications
Eastbourne, East Sussex BN23 6NT, England

The graphic circle C logo is a registered trademark of David C Cook.

Scripture information can be found on page 96.

ISBN 978-1-56292-762-2

Manuscript compiled by W.B. Freeman Concepts, Inc.
Tulsa, Oklahoma

Manufactured in Shen Zhen, Guang Dong, P.R. China,
in October 2011 by Printplus Limited.
First Edition 1999

10 11 12 13 14 15 16 17 18

102011

Illustrations by Julie Sawyer

A Note to Parents

Millions of children have enjoyed the *God's Little Instruction Book for Kids* series. Now we've coupled their favorite quotes and Scriptures with adorable four-color illustrations and put them into this perfect size for little hands.

Your children will love to carry this tiny book around with them in their pockets or backpacks, keep it handy in their desks, share it with their friends, and retreat to their favorite spots to read it over and over. God's Word comes alive in this mini-edition, which includes tidbits of wisdom from scriptures, rhymes, and quotes.

Read it to your children, or have them read it to you, and ask them what they think each saying means. It's a great, simple, and fun way to hide God's love and wisdom in your children's hearts!

See others as God sees them. See yourself as God sees you!

Do not think of anyone as the world does. . . . If anyone belongs to Christ, then he is made new.
(2 Corinthians 5:16-17)

Finish what you start.

Finishing is better than starting!
(Ecclesiastes 7:8 TLB)

A quitter never wins. A winner never quits!

I run straight for the finish line. (1 Corinthians 9:26 GNB)

Of all the things you keep, keep your word.

God always keeps his word.
(Psalms 146:6 CEV)

16

God is always in the mood to hear a song from you.

Shout for joy to the LORD, all the
earth, burst into jubilant
song with music.
(Psalms 98:4 NIV)

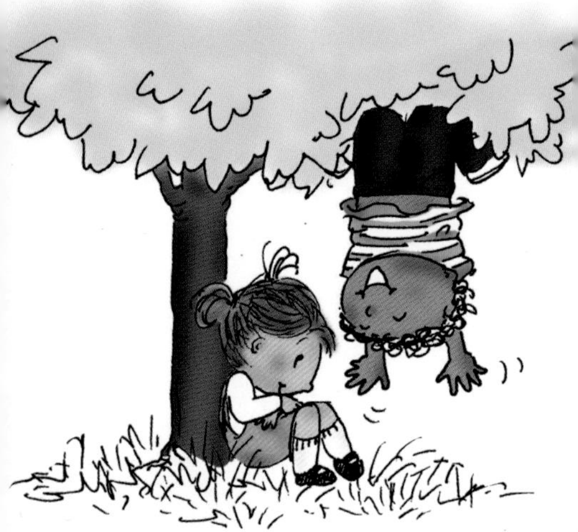

Need cheering up?
Cheer up
somebody else!

Kind words bring life.
(Proverbs 15:4 GNB)

Whatever you choose to be, choose to be good in God's eyes.

Do your best to be pure and faultless in God's sight and to be at peace with him.
(2 Peter 3:14 GNB)

Always tell the truth. That way you don't have to remember what you've said!

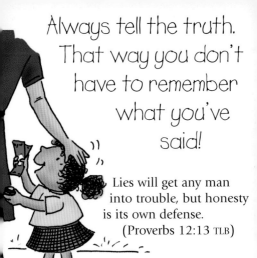

Lies will get any man into trouble, but honesty is its own defense.
(Proverbs 12:13 TLB)

A real friend always tells the truth.

An honest answer is a sign
of true friendship.
(Proverbs 24:26 GNB)

Give with a smile!

God loves a cheerful giver.
(2 Corinthians 9:7 NKJV)

25

The best chance to take
is the chance to do
something nice for
another person.

Use every chance you have
for doing good.
(Ephesians 5:16)

It's never too late to forgive.

Forgive, and you will be forgiven.
(Luke 6:37 NKJV)

Avoid following the crowd. Be an engine— not a caboose.

The LORD will make you the
head and not the tail.
(Deuteronomy 28:13 NKJV)

This gift doesn't cost anything, doesn't make noise, and doesn't need batteries. One size fits all. It's ideal for all ages. And it can always be returned. What is it?
A HUG!

Love each other with brotherly affection.
(Romans 12:10 TLB)

For You

XOXOXOXOX

Please don't get too upset with me. I'm still under construction!

Man looks at the outward
appearance, but the LORD
looks at the heart.
(1 Samuel 16:7 NIV)

You don't have to wait until you grow up to be a missionary. Tell some-one about Jesus today!

Don't let anyone look down on you because you are young, but set an example for the believers in speech, in life, in love, in faith and in purity.
(1 Timothy 4:12 NIV)

A thankful heart is a happy heart.

In everything give thanks.
(1 Thessalonians 5:18 NKJV)

Recipe for a good life: Just add Jesus.

Depend on the LORD. Trust him,
and he will take care of you.
(Psalms 37:5)

What's the "good" word? God's Word— the Bible!

Your word is like a lamp for my feet
and a light for my way.
(Psalms 119:105)

You don't need matches to be on fire for God!

Do not be lazy but work hard.
Serve the Lord with all your heart.
(Romans 12:11)

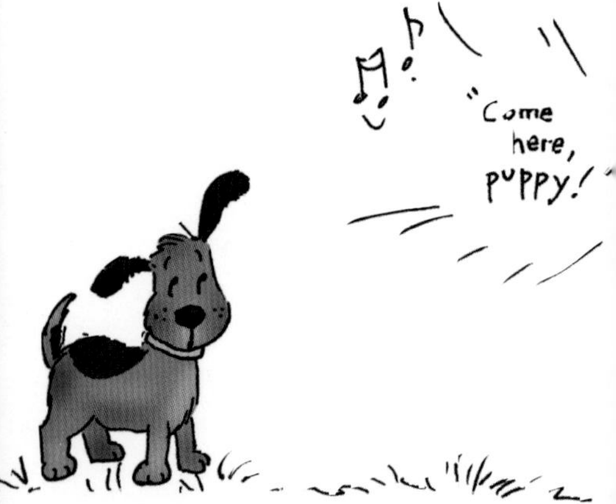
"Come here, puppy!"

When you listen, you learn.

My child, listen to your father's teaching. And do not forget your mother's advice.
(Proverbs 1:8)

"Good boy!"

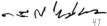

When God forgives you, it's like giving your soul a good bubble bath.

Wash away all my guilt
and make me clean again.
(Psalms 51:2)

There's no place like home.

For we know that when this tent we
live in now is taken down . . . we will
have wonderful new bodies in
heaven, homes that will be
ours forevermore.
(2 Corinthians 5:1 TLB)

J =

O =

Y =

JOY is found in putting
Jesus first.
Others second.
Yourself last.

This is what God commands: that we
believe in his Son, Jesus Christ,
and that we love each other.
(1 John 3:23)

• J O Y • J O Y • J O Y •

When Jesus knocks on the door of your heart—LET HIM IN!

Look! I have been standing at the door . . . knocking. If anyone . . . opens the door, I will come in and fellowship with him and he with me. (Revelation 3:20 TLB)

Children are some of Jesus' favorite friends!

Let the little children come to me,
and do not hinder them, for the
kingdom of God belongs
to such as these.
(Mark 10:14 NIV)

I love you, Jesus!

Learn to smile EVEN when there's a hole in your umbrella!

He calms the storm.
(Psalms 107:29 NKJV)

Tomorrow is a brand-new blank page. Draw something beautiful on it!

I will give you a new heart and put
a new spirit in you.
(Ezekiel 36:26 NIV)

Love is the glue that holds families together.

You should be like one big happy family, full of sympathy toward each other, loving one another with tender hearts and humble minds.
(1 Peter 3:8 TLB)

I LOVE YOU

A good time to say
"I love you" to someone
you care about is—
ANY time!

All people will know that you are my
followers if you love each other.
(John 13:35)

You can always share your secrets with God in prayer. He knows how to keep a secret forever.

He knows the secrets of every heart. (Psalms 44:21 TLB)

Even little people
can do big things.

I can do all things through Christ
because he gives me strength.
(Philippians 4:13)

Make the person you see in the mirror each morning one of your best buddies.

For in the image of God has God made man.
(Genesis 9:6 NIV)

69

Be a good worker.

The work of his hands
rewards him.
(Proverbs 12:14 NIV)

72

Flowers are love notes from God.

Flowers appear on the earth;
the season of singing has
come, the cooing of
doves is heard in
our land.
(Song of Songs 2:12 NIV)

Doing something nice for someone is like giving him a cup of hot cocoa on a cold winter's day.

Being kind to the poor is like lending to the LORD. The LORD will reward you for what you have done.
(Proverbs 19:17)

74

Everybody ought to know, everybody ought to know, everybody ought to know Who Jesus is!

"Who do you say I am?" Peter answered, "You are the Christ." (Mark 8:29 NIV)

The best thing to do to someone who hurts you is to do a nice thing in return.

Love your enemies. Do good to those who hate you.
(Luke 6:27 TLB)

Learning how to lose
is the first step
to becoming a
good winner.

And let us run with perseverance
the race marked out for us.
(Hebrews 12:1 NIV)

Every person has a Jesus-shaped hole in his heart.

My soul yearns for you in the night; in the morning my spirit longs for you.
(Isaiah 26:9 NIV)

Never, never, NEVER
give up on a friend.

A friend loves at all times, and a
brother is born for adversity.
(Proverbs 17:17 NIV)

The Mustard See

Even a little faith can result in a big miracle.

If you had faith even as small as a tiny mustard seed you could say to this mountain, "Move!" and it would go far away.
(Matthew 17:20 TLB)

When nobody is around to hold your hand, remember that God is holding you in His hand.

My hand will sustain him;
surely my arm will
strengthen him.
(Psalms 89:21 NIV)

When you want to do what God wants you to do, He will help you do it! Ask Him!

I am your God. I will make you strong and will help you.
(Isaiah 41:10)

90

Weeds can't grow in places where you have planted flowers.

Do not be overcome by evil, but overcome evil with good. (Romans 12:21 NIV)

When you help someone else, you help yourself.

He who refreshes others
will himself
be refreshed.
(Proverbs 11:25 NIV)

Sawyer

84

Little people can still have big hearts.

Seek first the kingdom of God and His righteousness, and all these things shall be added to you.
(Matthew 6:33 NKJV)